MEL BAY

CHILDREN'S SONGS FOR
MADE EASY
BY ROSS NICKERSON

MW00794830

1 2 3 4 5 6 7 8 9 0

Visit us on the Web at www.melbay.com — E-mail us at email@melbay.com

CD Track Sheet

Banjo only/Faster Version

1/Medly: She'll Be Coming' Round the Mountain, Oh Susanna, Sailor's Hornpipe, Turkey in the Straw
2/Turkey in the Straw
3/Skip to My Lou
4/This Old Man
5/Shortnin' Bread
6/Frere Jacques
7/Eensy Weensy Spider
8/Wheels on the Bus
9/London Bridge
10/Old MacDonald
11/ Mary Had a Little Lamb
12/Twinkle Little Star
13/She'll Be Comin' Round the Mountain
14/Froggy Went a Courtin
15/Camptown Races
16/Workin' on the Railroad
17/ Farmer in the Dell
18/ Sailor's Hornpipe
19/ On Top of Old Smoky
20/ Three Blind Mice
21/ Oh Susanna
22/ Bah, Bah Black Sheep
23/ Row Your Boat
24/ Rock a Bye Baby

Note: Each song is recorded at three different speeds with a separate rhythm track to play along with. The medium speed on each song also has the banjo lead track in one channel and the rhythm track in the opposite channel. Away in a Manger and Silent Night are only recorded at two speeds because the tempos are slower.

Turkey in the Straw
25 Medium speed
26 Slower speed
27 Up Tempo

Skip to My Lou
28 Medium speed
29 Slower speed
30 Up Tempo

This Old Man
31 Medium speed
32 Slower speed

Shortnin' Bread
33 Medium speed
34 Slower speed
35 Up Tempo

Frere Jaques
36 Medium speed
37 Slower speed

Eensy Weensy Spider
38 Medium speed
39 Slower speed

Wheels on the Bus
40 Medium speed
41 Slower speed
42 Up Tempo

London Bridge
43 Medium speed
44 Slower speed

Old MacDonald
45 Medium speed
46 Slower speed
47 Up Tempo

Mary Had a Little Lamb
48 Medium speed
49 Slower speed
50 Up Tempo

Twinkle, Twinkle Little Star
51 Medium speed
52 Slower speed

She'll Be Comin' Round the Mountain
53 Medium speed
54 Slower speed
55 Up Tempo

Froggy Went a Courtin'
56 Medium speed
57 Slower speed
58 Up Tempo

Camptown Races
59 Medium speed
60 Slower speed
61 Up Tempo

Workin' on the Railroad
62 Medium speed
63 Slower speed
64 Up Tempo

Farmer in the Dell
65 Medium speed
66 Slower speed

Sailor's Hornpipe
67 Medium speed
68 Slower speed
69 Up Tempo

On Top of Old Smoky
70 Medium speed
71 Slower speed

Three Blind Mice
72 Medium speed
73 Slower speed
74 Up Tempo

Oh Susanna
75 Medium speed
76 Slower speed
77 Up Tempo

Bah Bah Black Sheep
78 Medium speed
79 Slower speed
80 Up Tempo

Row, Row, Row your Boat
81 Medium speed
82 Slower speed

Rock a Bye Baby
83 Medium speed
84 Slower speed

All Banjo Tracks were played by Ross Nickerson and recorded by Bill Cashman, at the Cavern Studios in Tucson, AZ March, 2005.

Children's Songs for Banjo Made Easy
by Ross Nickerson
TABLE OF CONTENTS

About the Author
Ross Nickerson

Ross Nickerson has recorded with some of the top names in Bluegrass music. His skills were just featured on a compilation CD called *Ultimate Banjo* that included banjo legends, Earl Scruggs and Sonny Osborne. Ross recently appeared on stage with The Riders in the Sky and The Oak Ridge Boys and has picked and appeared with many of the best banjo players in the world including Earl Scruggs, Bela Fleck and Ralph Stanley. Ross's CD *Blazing the West* has won several awards including being named by Country Music Television as one of the top ten CDs to pick up in 2003. Ross has just completed a new CD called *Let's Kick Some Ass* that features his hard driving bluegrass banjo style and own personal touch. Throughout his career Ross Nickerson has always enjoyed sharing his knowledge and helping others to learn to play the banjo. His many years of experience teaching privately and traveling the world to hold group workshops has helped him gain many unique insights into the common obstacles facing banjo students today. He has listened to his students, seen the challenges they face, understands what students are craving for and always delivers his practical, focused instruction in a personable and easy to follow manner. Ross Nickerson is the author of the top selling banjo book, *The Banjo Encyclopedia "Bluegrass Banjo from A to Z"*. He has also written and recorded many other books, CDs and DVDs designed to help banjo students save time and learn the fun of playing 5-string banjo easier. Ross is a full time musician and on the road ten to fifteen days a month performing concerts, teaching banjo workshops and reaching new audiences. He has been selected as a faculty member for many prestigious bluegrass and banjo camps and is the founder and coordinator of the Nova Scotia Banjo Camp and the annual BanjoTeacher.com Banjo Cruise. Find Ross at his website BanjoTeacher.com.

Ackowledgements

Thanks to Mel Bay for publishing my instructional books, CDs and DVDs and believing in my work.

Thanks to Michael Namorato for doing a final edit on my text.

Many, many thanks to my students, friends and family for their support!

http://banjoteacher.com
http://rossnickerson.com

Foreword

Thanks for purchasing Children's Songs for Banjo Made Easy! I designed the arrangements to bring out the melody, as well as making it easy enough for a beginner or intermediate player to learn the arrangements pretty quickly.

I hope you like the arrangements. I took great care to make the arrangements easy to learn and play. As in any banjo arrangement you learn there is normally more than one way to play any particular song. If you want to change something to fit what you hear or like you, as a student, should do so. If, however, you venture off, keep your technique solid. Technique is much less subjective and as a student you should not be reinventing the three-finger Scruggs style approach. For instance: If I indicate an index finger on the fretting hand and the middle is working for you, that's your choice. However, be careful not to use that as an excuse to have anarchy in the fretting hand. Try to be sensible in your approach with respect to minimized movement etc. The picking hand is less subjective and the indications in the tab I recommend be adhered to. If you are venturing off from the written tab, try to keep your picking hand technique solid and be sure to **not** use the same finger for consecutive eighth notes.

If you haven't mastered counting and understanding the relationship between quarter and eighth notes you will have a great deal of difficulty playing these arrangements. I use quarter notes often for the melody note so they will stand out. I can't bring myself to write arrangements that are all eighth notes because they sound monotonous and the melody is often buried, especially if the student is not skilled in accenting.

I recommend learning to count, tap, or beat out the rhythm of the songs you are learning without playing the banjo first, especially if you are having trouble with timing. Remember, the melody notes are only half of what you are reading, the other is the time value of the note. Without the correct time value of each note executed properly, the melody will not appear in the right place.

As a banjo teacher I spend much of my private lesson time with students straightening out poor timing execution and poor fretting-hand technique. So, if you are learning these without a teacher, take that into account and give those areas special attention.

Thanks for reading my suggestions and good luck!

Sincerely, Ross Nickerson

Mel Bay Publications

How to Read Tablature

Each horizontal line of the music staff represents a string on the banjo.

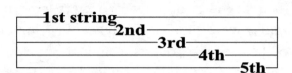

In the songs we will be learning there are four beats in each measure. A measure is the space between the lines. The 4/4 indicates the song has four quarter beats in each measure.

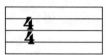

If there is a 0 on the line, you play that string open. The number on the line is the fret you play with the left hand.

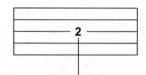

The picking finger is indicated under the note you're picking, below the tab lines.

Fretting hand indications are under the note and circled as shown below.

T = thumb	I = index	M = middle

① = index	② = middle	③ = ring	④ = little

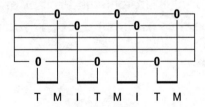
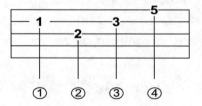

>

Symbol for accenting or emphasizing a note

Timing in the tablature is indicated with stems coming off the notes. The notes with only a single stem are quarter notes. The notes with the stems connected by bars are eighth notes. Sixteenth notes are connected by two bars.

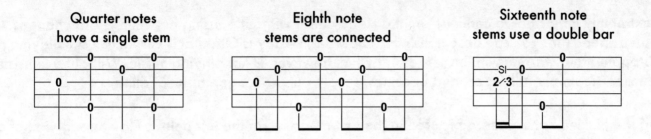

The chord of the measure you are playing is indicated above the tab. The chord stays the same until another chord is indicated.

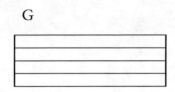

When you see dots like pictured below in the music, it means to repeat. When you reach the dots on the right, repeat back to the dots on the left.

In some cases, first and second endings are used. After repeating once, skip the FIRST ENDING, then play the SECOND ENDING and continue on in the song.

Here are the indications for slides, hammer-ons, and pull-offs.

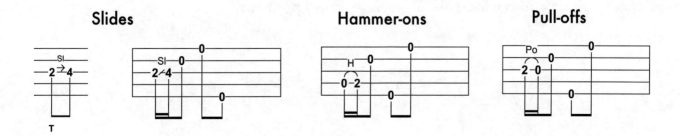

Learning the Chords to Each Song

I highly recommend learning the chords to each song BEFORE you begin memorizing and learning the song from tablature in the fashion presented below. What you will see below is called a chord chart or could be referred to as, simply writing out the chords to the song. This is a standard and recommended procedure in bluegrass music.

It is extremely important to continue on at a steady beat without pausing between chord changes. Go only at a speed that you can accomplish this. Slow and steady is OK, that is very much still playing music. Stopping and starting with no sense of rhythm, however, is not playing music. Without a consistent rhythm, music simply falls apart and becomes, simply put, no longer music at all.

Using the picking-hand pattern pictured in the first measure on the left below. Play through the chord changes for "She'll be Coming Around the Mountain" all the way through at least 4 times without stopping. Do not pause or break your steady rhythm between the chord changes. SLOW IS OK, STOPPING IN THE MIDDLE OF SONG IS NOT. Next, play through the chord changes with one of the one measure rolls pictured below, or you could use another one measure roll of your choice.

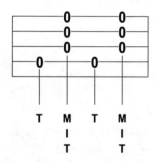 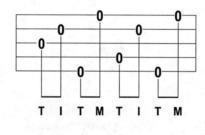 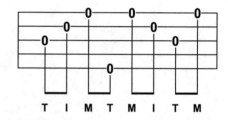

/= one measure (For each / you would play one of the measures pictured above)

She'll Be Coming Around the Mountain

G   D G C G D G

////// // // // / / //

After you have mastered the chords lower on the neck in the basic chord shapes for the songs you are learning, at a later time it would be very good practice to return to the chord charts and take it a step further by playing the chords to these songs up the neck using the F form, D form and Barre form chord shapes. If you are not familiar with these chord shapes yet, please refer to my book, The Banjo Encyclopedia where you can learn these movable chord positions.

More on Learning the Chords and Memorizing

Next, begin memorizing the song. When you are playing the song by memory, if you lose your place (which can be expected, everyone does) you can fall back on playing the roll I gave you on the previous page or another simple roll while holding the correct chords until you recover the melody. This will not stop the beat and is far more effective than stopping to correct your mistake. This simple concept of continuing picking while holding the correct chord and not breaking your rhythm could save you years of practice time. Maintaining a beat in your music should be your primary goal as a banjo player.

If you cannot play a difficult section of a song, correct it by isolating the difficult spot and then cycle the measure or phrase over and over in time until it becomes easier. Once that is accomplished, you can now place it back into the song in rhythm without stumbling or losing the beat.

These recommendations should help you overcome and maintain crucial aspects in your banjo playing progress such as recovering from mistakes, playing with others, being able to play along with songs you don't know and, most importantly, moving you forward in the most efficient use of your practice time.

More Memorizing Tips

■   When learning from tablature, memorizing the song or section of tablature that you are learning is the very first thing you should do. Tablature is not intended to be sight read. It is a great way of writing down music to make it easier to memorize.

■   Repeat short phrases (between 1 and 3 measures) over and over and immediately try to play them by memory by simply turning the tab over.

■   Identify the spots you keep forgetting and repeat them ten times as much, or more!

■   Play the song without the tab as soon as you can. When you are absolutely sure you can't remember a spot, then open the book and take a peek.

■   Memorize the chords to each song you learn. It is like having an outline or a road map to help you find your place at all times. Writing down the chords to the song on a separate piece of paper is an excellent approach for memorizing them.

These are just a few more suggestions, but they may help. I'm sure if you make a conscious effort to memorize you will come up with some methods of your own. Simply put, the best way to accomplish playing your banjo without a dependency on tablature is to close the book and practice without it often.

Note: It is not realistic to play these arrangements exactly as they are written without losing your place, even after a lot of practice. Learn to fall back on steady picking and the chords! We all do! In addition, focus on learning solid 5-string bluegrass banjo right and left-hand techniques, (learn the proper timing, and use the correct picking and fretting fingers.) If you learn to play the banjo properly, when you make a mistake, your default technique will be solid and you will be able to cover the mistake more seamlessly.

Tips for Learning Each Song

By using some of my tips and suggestions I'm confident that I can help you make better use of your practice time and achieve progress quicker. It's important to keep in mind that your goal is to be able to physically play the song as well as to learn and remember it. You must either already have the skill to play the song effectively before you learn it, or build skill during the learning process. Here are some suggestions that I believe will help you cut to the chase in practice sessions and help you to stay out of a "sight reading the tab rut" that could be easy to fall in to.

Breaking the song into separate areas of practice and focus

Learn the frets, positions and correct fingers on the fretting hand without picking.
Read through the tablature without picking to find the different frets, chords or positions you will use during the song. As you find your way with the fretting hand, proceed slowly, fret accurately, and use the correct fretting fingers indicated in the tab. This will build up muscle memory, ability, coordination and skill in your fretting hand and be a quicker way to memorize the song. A metronome would be extremely helpful in this process.

Count out the timing of the notes played by the picking hand without picking first.
Tap out with a pencil or count out loud the timing of the notes in the picking hand before you begin trying to play the song. This is an extremely effective way of learning a song and I believe if you take the time to do this you will learn the song quicker and become a better banjo player in the long run. If you do not take a moment to master this and learn to count the time between 1/4 and 1/8th notes correctly I'm afraid that no amount of hitting the correct fret or string will help you from being in the wrong place in the song. As someone who has taught private lessons a long time I have found that I spend much of the students lesson time correcting improper timing of notes. Generally speaking, students do not work on this on their own, they gravitate their attention primarily to the correct string or fret with no regard to the timing of the notes. The timing of the notes is extremely important. Learn to count, it's easy and fun too. My book The Banjo Encyclopedia from Mel Bay covers this in more depth.

Read through the tab and identify the most difficult segments in the song and work on them the most.
It's realistic that some parts of an arrangement will take you as much as 50 to 100 times more practice to master. If you do not repeat the hard parts 100 times, you will have to play the whole song 100 times, and even then, that does not work as well as really attacking the hard parts with repetition.

Be able to play through the chord changes of the song with a simple roll before beginning to learn the song using tablature.
This could be the single most helpful thing you can do for your progress and sense of enjoyment. If you are able to achieve this before you learn the tablature for song, you will always have a place to go if you lose your place in the arrangement which will keep you from having a stop or break your rhythm. Keeping a steady beat with your picking should always be your top priority as a banjo player.

Look for repeated sections or phrases in the song, cycle them over and over and build up ability as well as muscle memory in them.
These are freebies, always look for repeated phrases or even sections that are only slightly different. This not only makes the learning and memorizing process easier, it's great for killing two birds with one stone while concentrating on skill building in a single section.

Listen to the CD recording while following along with the tablature, without playing.
While doing this, focus on learning the timing of the picking hand and how the arrangement is put together as a whole. Think your way through the song while listening, this can be very effective and save you valuable practice time.

Turkey in the Straw

Key of G
Traditional
Arrangement: Ross Nickerson

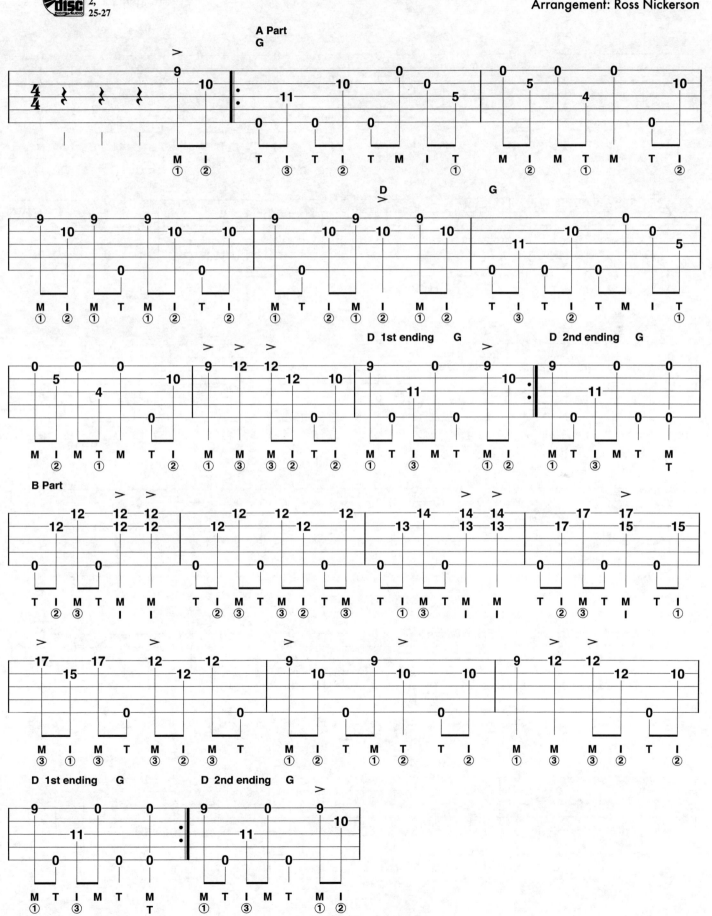

Skip to My Lou

Key of G
Traditional
Arrangement: Ross Nickerson

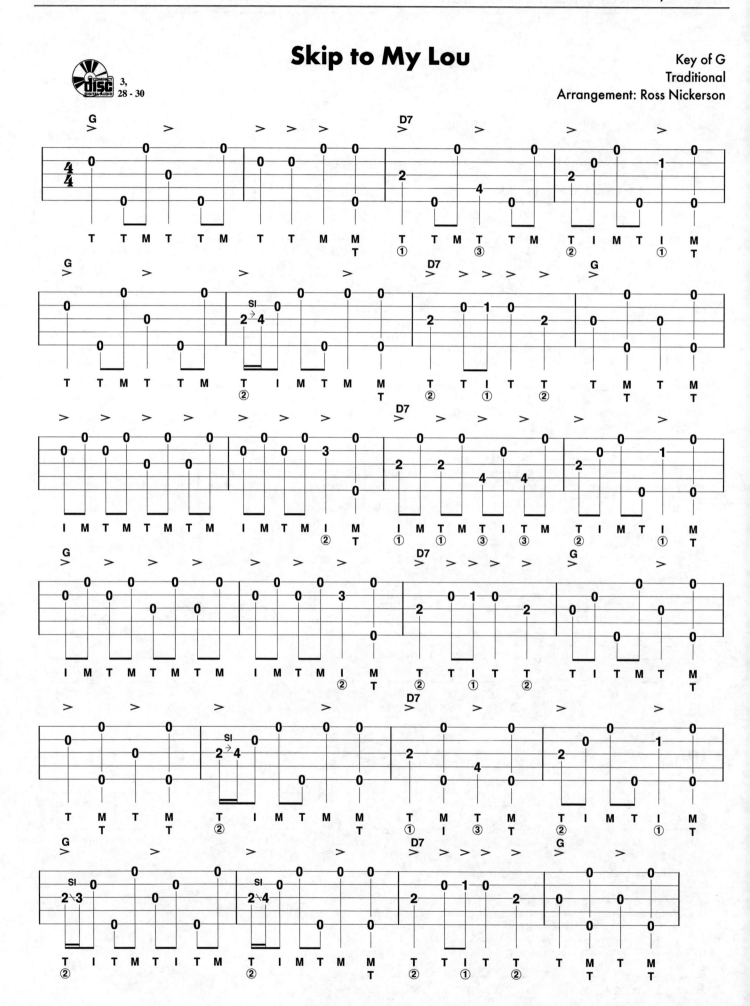

This Old Man

Key of G
Traditional
Arrangement: Ross Nickerson

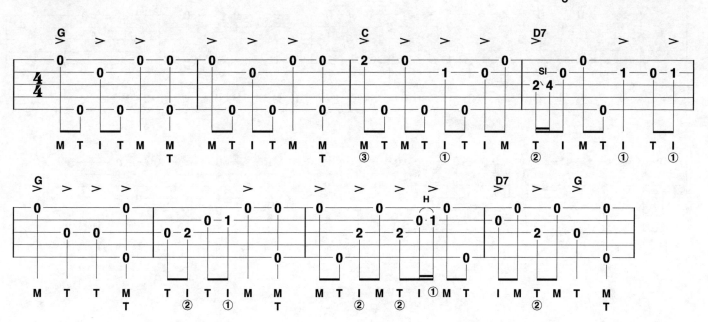

Shortin' Bread

Key of G
Traditional
Arrangement: Ross Nickerson

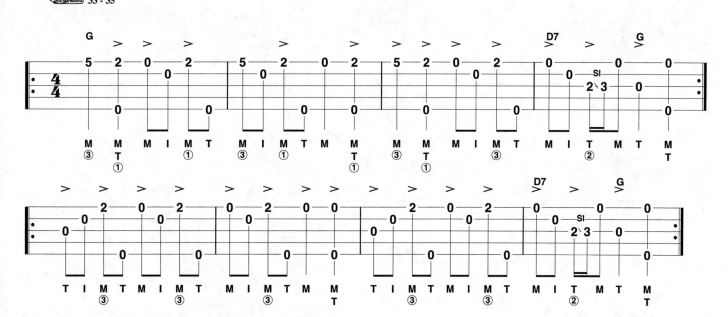

Frere Jacques

Key of G
Traditional
Arrangement: Ross Nickerson

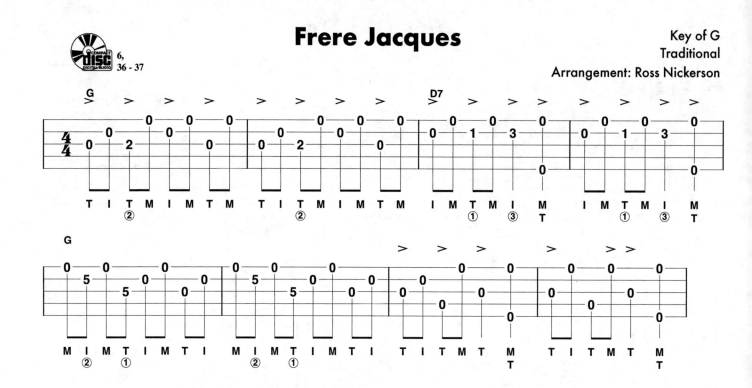

Eensy Weensy Spider

Key of G
Traditional
Arrangement: Ross Nickerson

Wheels on the Bus

Key of G
Traditional
Arrangement: Ross Nickerson

London Bridge

Key of G
Traditional
Arrangement: Ross Nickerson

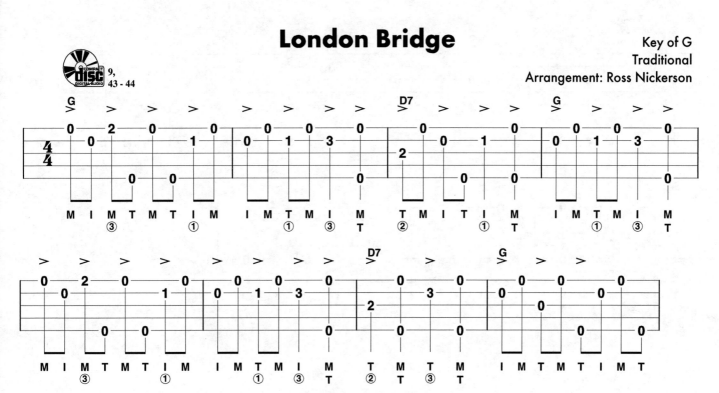

Old MacDonald

Key of G
Traditional
Arrangement: Ross Nickerson

Mary Had a Little Lamb

Key of G
Traditional
Arrangement: Ross Nickerson

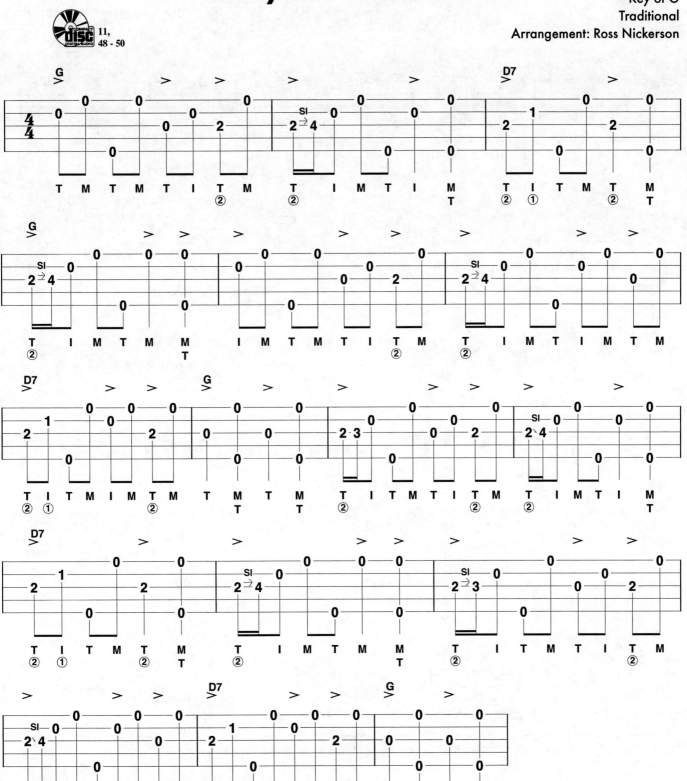

Twinkle, Twinkle Little Star

Key of G
Traditional
Arrangement: Ross Nickerson

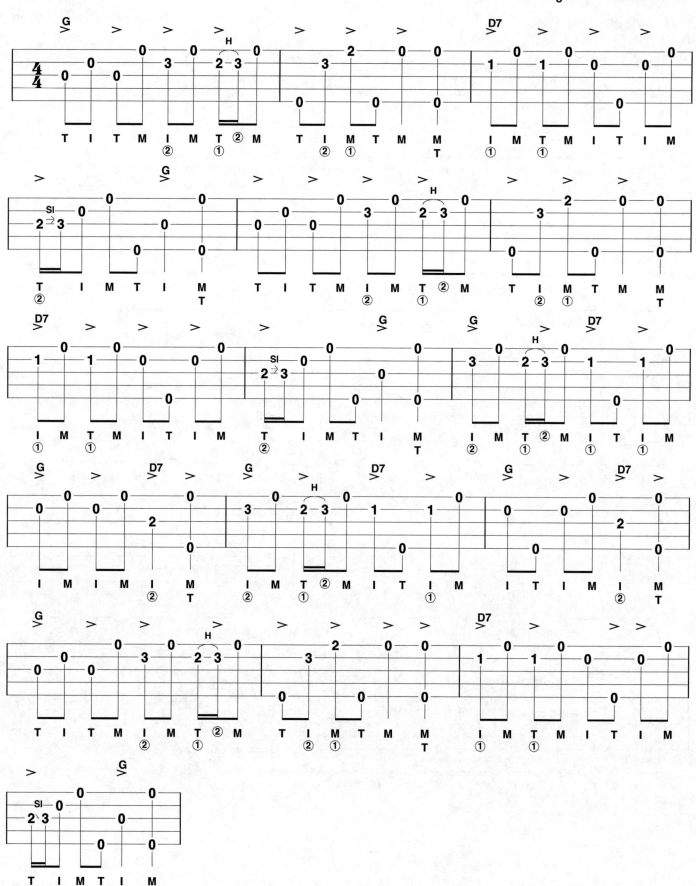

She'll Be Comin' Round the Mountain

Key of G
Traditional
Arrangement: Ross Nickerson

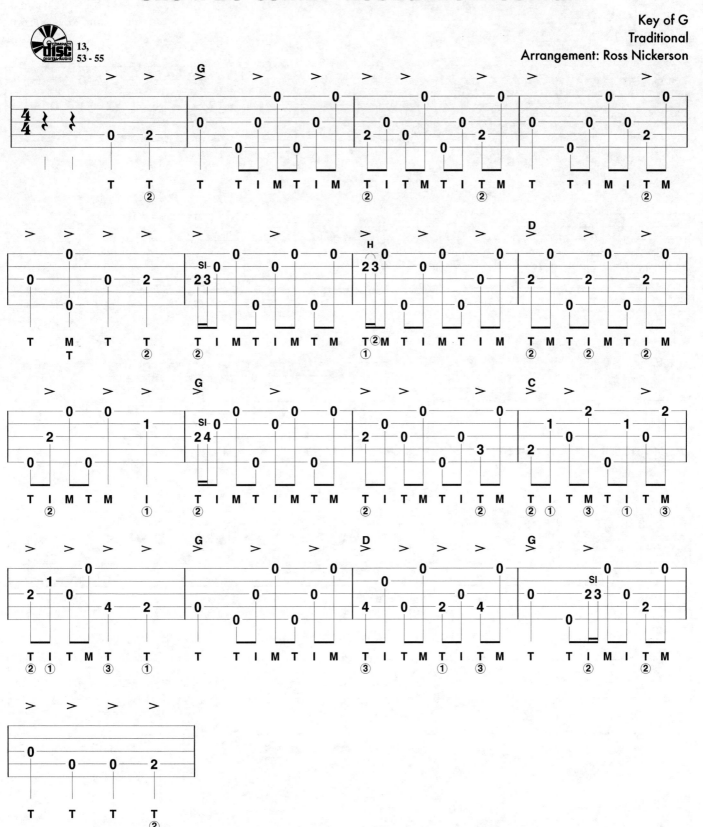

Froggy Went a Courtin'

Key of G
Traditional
Arrangement: Ross Nickerson

Camptown Races

Key of G
Traditional
Arrangement: Ross Nickerson

Workin' on the Railroad

Key of G
Traditional
Arrangement: Ross Nickerson

Workin' on the Railroad (page 2)

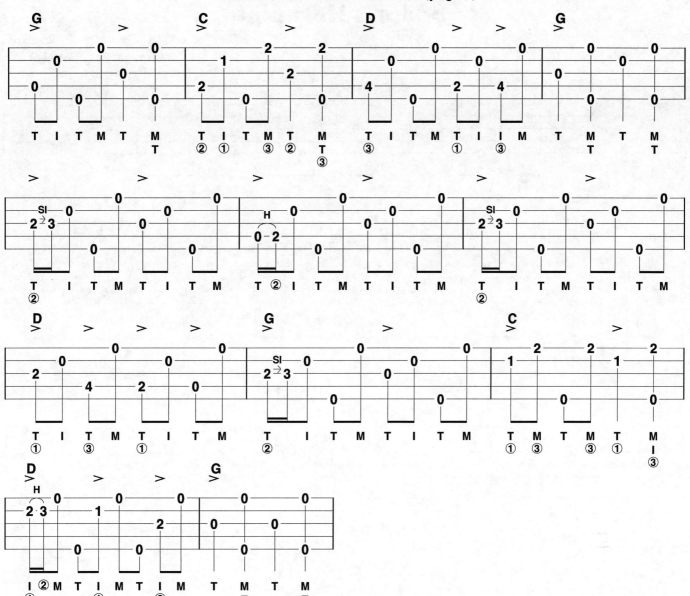

Farmer in the Dell

Key of G
Traditional
Arrangement: Ross Nickerson

17,
65 - 66

Sailor's Hornpipe

Key of G
Traditional
Arrangement: Ross Nickerson

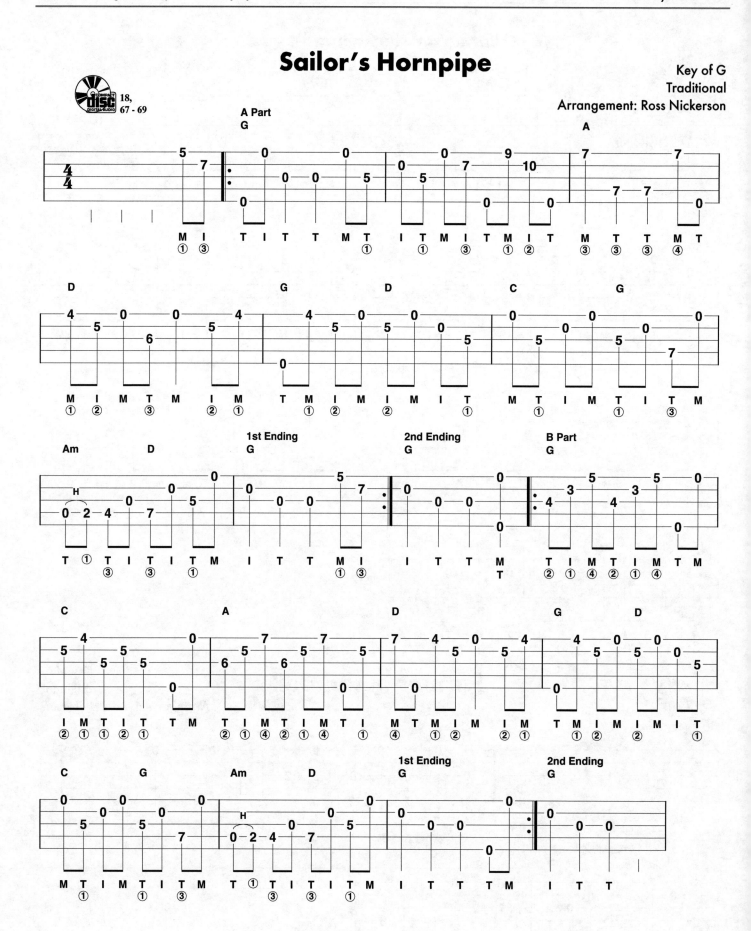

On Top of Old Smoky

Key of G
Traditional
Arrangement: Ross Nickerson

**Ross Nickerson
in concert
2003**

Three Blind Mice

Key of G
Traditional
Arrangement: Ross Nickerson

Mel Bay Publications

Oh Susanna

Key of G
Traditional
Arrangement: Ross Nickerson

Bah Bah Black Sheep

Key of Em
Traditional
Arrangement: Ross Nickerson

Row, Row, Row Your Boat

Key of G
Traditional
Arrangement: Ross Nickerson

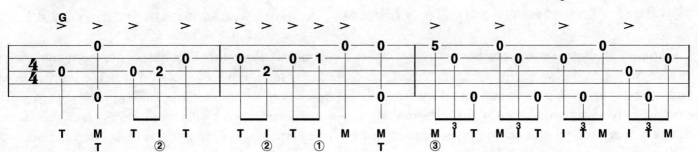

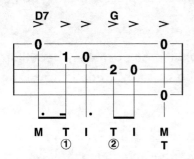

Rock a Bye Baby

Key of G
Traditional
Arrangement: Ross Nickerson

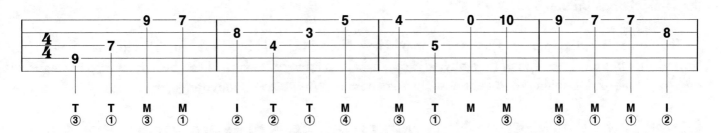

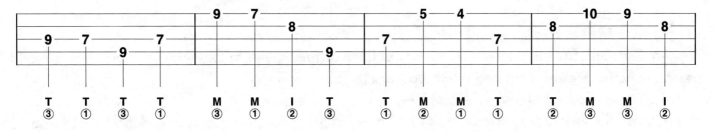

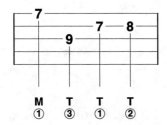

Other Mel Bay Books
by Ross Nickerson

The Banjo Encyclopedia by Ross Nickerson "Bluegrass Banjo from A to Z"

The Banjo Encyclopedia is a comprehensive, in-depth banjo instructional tool that covers the many intricacies of bluegrass banjo playing, including numerous topics that may have been overlooked in banjo instruction to date. *The Banjo Encyclopedia* can take a student from the beginning, to intermediate, and right through to more advanced styles of banjo playing. This wide-ranging banjo instructional book will focus on many techniques that will help every aspect of a banjo player's musicianship while simplifying many subjects in the learning process and comes with a 99 track CD. *The Banjo Encyclopedia* is undoubtedly one of the most complete five-string banjo books on the market today and a must for every banjo player's collection.

....I think that what you have created is the new gold standard for banjo instruction. It is an absolutely beautiful, beautifully written book, which I know will now be the foundation of my lifetime banjo study. I don't know how it could possibly be any better.

...I got it Friday and have read it cover to cover. Very well done. ...I did go to the Table of Contents and, in my opinion as a former HS teacher and college lecturer for 25 years - Ross has put together something that I would say is the first book/CD that anyone who knows they want to learn 5 string should have.

.....bought your Banjo Encyclopaedia about 6 weeks ago, I have put all my other books on ice, yours is THE one. It covers everything I will possibly want to know for the next 20 years or so. It will in my opinion become the seminal book on banjo.

.....The Banjo Encyclopedia is more than I dreamed it would be. I could have saved myself a lot of money if I had started with this one book rather than buying 4 or 5 others to figure out which I liked best. Ross is so professional and so in tune with beginner and intermediate weaknesses. What a great teacher.

Other Titles Released or Upcoming from Ross Nickerson and Mel Bay

Christmas Music for Banjo Made Easy by Ross Nickerson
Popular Christmas favorites written out in easy and fun arrangements to play. The book includes the songs demonstrated at three speeds and a backup track to play along with.

Fiddle Tunes for Banjo Made Easy by Ross Nickerson
This book is laid out in a similar fashion as Children's Songs for Banjo Made Easy and includes 14 popular fiddle tunes! As in all the books in this series, the CD includes a backup track to play along with!

Bluegrass Standards for Banjo Made Easy by Ross Nickerson
Another in a series of books from Mel Bay and Ross Nickerson to make it easy for banjo students to learn new songs and progress with their technique!

Gospel Songs for Banjo Made Easy by Ross Nickerson
Bluegrass Banjo arrangements of Gospel classics. A great way for you to learn the technique of how to play melodies on the five-string banjo, while also learning these excellent arrangements.